A Cloudy Day

by Robin Nelson

first step nonfiction

It is a cloudy day!

Clouds fill the sky.

Some clouds are
thin and high.

Some clouds are
flat and low.

Some clouds are **puffy.**

Some clouds touch
the **ground.**

Clouds can be white.

Clouds can be gray.

When it is cloudy,
water fills the sky.

Rain and snow fall.

When it is cloudy, we see
shadows of clouds.

Clouds cover the sun.

When it is cloudy,
mountains hide.

Planes fly over the clouds.

When it is cloudy, we look
for pictures in the sky.

A cloudy day is fun!

Types of Clouds

Cirrus clouds
are thin, white
clouds that are
very high
in the sky.

Stratus clouds are flat, gray
clouds that are low in the sky.
Stratus clouds sometimes look
like layers of clouds.

Cumulus clouds are puffy. Cumulus clouds can be big or small. Cumulus clouds can be white or gray.

Fog is a cloud that forms close to the ground.

Cloudy Day Facts

Clouds are made of very small droplets of water and dust.

The color of a cloud tells you how much water is inside. A very dark cloud holds a lot of water droplets. The darker the cloud, the harder it is going to rain!

Thunderclouds can form as high as 10 to 11 miles above the earth.

It will probably rain if cumulus clouds are high in the sky or if there are many different types of clouds in the sky at the same time.

You can create your own cloud on a cold day. Just breathe into the cold air. Do you see the cloud?

A cumulus cloud can hold about 25 gallons of water.

Glossary

 clouds – masses of water droplets or ice crystals floating in the air

 flat – smooth and even

 ground – the surface of the earth

 puffy – soft, light, and fluffy

 shadows – darks shapes made by something blocking light

Index

The photographs in this book are reproduced through the courtesy of: © Richard Cummins, front cover, pp. 2, 8, 9, 10, 15, 18 (top), 19 (top); © Michele Burgess, pp. 3, 4, 7, 13, 14, 22 (top); © Jeff Greenberg/Photo Network, pp. 5, 22 (2nd from top); © Steve Foley/Independent Picture Service, pp. 6, 22 (2nd from bottom); © Betty Crowell, pp. 11, 12, 19 (bottom), 22 (center and bottom); © Doug Crouch/CORBIS, p. 16; © Raymond Gehman/CORBIS, p. 17; © Wisconsin Department of Natural Resources, p. 18 (bottom).

This book is available in two editions:
Library binding by Lerner Publications Company, a division of Lerner Publishing Group
Soft cover by First Avenue Editions, an imprint of Lerner Publishing Group
241 First Avenue North
Minneapolis, MN 55401 U.S.A.

Website address: www.lernerbooks.com

LIBRARY OF CONGRESS CATALOGING-IN-PUBLICATION DATA

Nelson, Robin.
    A cloudy day / by Robin Nelson.
        p.   cm. — (First step nonfiction)
    Includes index.
    ISBN 0-8225-0172-4 (lib. bdg. : alk. paper)
    ISBN 0-8225-1961-5 (pbk. : alk. paper)
    1. Clouds—Juvenile literature. [1. Clouds.] I. Title. II. Series.
QC921.35.N45 2002
551.57'6—dc21   00-012943

Manufactured in the United States of America
1 2 3 4 5 6 – AM – 07 06 05 04 03 02